TRUST THE SIGNS

Create Your Best Life by
Learning the Language of Signs

Luisa Frey

This book is dedicated to:

The "village" that kept believing in me and my signs:

Diana, Dr. John, Theresa from Saratoga & Linda at Lamplight Inn, Lake Luzerne, NY.

And for my two "roses" who made me a firm believer in signs - my children Alex and Ethan

TABLE OF CONTENTS

Know the Signs
Luisa Frey

As I walked through miles of heartache and strife
I held on and am now rejoicing in a beautiful new life.

What things have made this rapturous change in me?
Could it be noticing the signs in all that I see?

I know now this is oh so very true
And soon others will learn this pearl of wisdom too

Of interpreting signs even though they are unspoken
For "sign" language fosters old habits to become broken.

Old energies become unhinged to make way for the new with glee
Now all that was challenging is just a distant memory to me.

The signs showed me the way all along my circuitous path
For signs cannot be computed, like formulas in science or math;

Instead they are felt, witnessed and seen
They are real, though some think they're a dream.

They come in all shapes, forms and modes

Yes, even in the form of musical odes!

So when you're observant for that which is repeatedly seen

You will start to know what sign language means.

Next step is to write down what you see, feel and suspect

For this will give you clarity and respect

Respect for the guiding force, which speaks to you through signs.

Next is to trust that the more you do this, the more your life aligns

Aligns so that you are where you're supposed to be.

Just wait to feel the taste of what it means to truly be free

Free of the "should haves," "what if's" and "what do I do?"

Because with signs, the language is tailored solely to YOU.

The signs are all around you, just pause to notice them all

And they will always support you and never let you fall.

There's a whole new language for you to learn

And it will quench your desire for what you yearn.

You are a butterfly, emerging from your old cocoon

With new and beautiful ways, to embrace you soon.

For butterflies transform to beings which gloriously flit about in flight

So let them lead you to your signs -- they'll forever shed their light!

PROLOGUE

We've all been there -- we see a number, a symbol, or literally a street sign that connects to something about which we have been thinking about. It is only natural to think of these signs as coincidences. However, if you keep track of the signs and personal symbols that you see on a regular basis, you will start to notice that there is a bit more to it than mere coincidence. By doing so, personal symbols and signs will become a language all their own that are individually tailored to you.

So why should you care about how signs and symbols can communicate with you? The fact is that signs can play a vital role in your life -- as they have in mine -- to help guide you through difficult times. Signs or personal symbols can affirm that you are on the right path and empower you to take steps towards change that might seem radical or illogical on the surface. By recognizing that you are receiving signs to help you make these changes, you are affirming that they are the right decisions to make--the universe, and your very soul, are telling you so!

Consider the wise words of global Deepak Chopra, who said, "There are no extra pieces in the universe. Everyone is here because he or she has a place to fill, and every piece must fit itself into the big jigsaw puzzle." We are all part of the complex fabric of the universe, and each of us plays a unique role in the great puzzle of life itself. There are always signs to guide us, as long as we are open to them.

I am living testimony that following the guidance of signs and personal symbols can lead to amazing, positive transformations. Over a period of twelve years, I filled up fifty-five journals with notes about my own personal symbols. Looking at these journals now affirms that this plethora of signs was no mere coincidence. Instead, it was guidance to help me transform from a caterpillar into a graceful butterfly, spreading her wings.

There are many parts of my life in which "sign language" has specifically guided me toward a happier, more peaceful and fulfilled life. For example, I followed my personal symbols to a path which included going back to college, getting an additional degree, learning a drastically new craft at the age of 52, and ultimately a major career change. Each time I took a big, scary step on this path, I was always supported and affirmed by my personal symbols. It was as if the signs were saying "keep going -- you are totally on the right path." And I was!

As a matter of fact, people who used to discount my personal symbols now text me and ask me for guidance on the meaning of the signs that *they* see. Even my children, who are 21 and 29 years-old at the time of writing *Trust the Signs*, used to roll their eyes when I would say, "Look, it's a sign!" Now, they even point out obvious displays of our personal symbols. All this has made me realize that all those years of recording my signs has not only helped me achieve a more fulfilling career, but it has also inspired others to take major steps in their lives toward greater happiness and financial security.

The goal of this book is for you to consider allowing signs and personal symbolism to become part of your mental and spiritual "tool kit" to empower you to take steps toward personal fulfillment. Each chapter is devised to lift your spirits with an inspirational poem, provide you with tips on how to read and follow your personal symbols and to entertain you as I weave in my own "no coincidence" stories of how the signs guided me.

The poems included here were all written before I made my career change. At the time that I wrote them, I was going through tremendous financial stress despite working very hard on my travel writing and social media business. The words in each poem came to me after I grew quiet in the early hours of the morning, during brief meditation. Since I always had my journals on hand to record the signs, I could quickly write down the inspirational poems that came out of me like a gushing waterfall. They helped me stay positive despite the grim reality of my life at the time. I am including some of them here to help lift you up to a place of positivity, inner strength and knowledge that, no matter how dire your situation may be, there is a guiding force* outside of us that can help us achieve a life of beauty and happiness. One of the many ways that this force manifests itself is through the appearance of signs and personal symbols in our daily lives.

Luisa Frey, August 22, 2023

*Note: It is entirely up to you as to whether you attribute the Divine orchestration of signs to God, the Universe, Spirit or any other force. Here, I will simply use the term "Divine orchestration," but feel free to substitute in your own belief system.

CHAPTER 1

THE ROSE

Seeds are Being Planted
Luisa Frey

You are a beautiful rose about to bloom

Just keep the faith -- it's happening so very soon!

You doubt the time frame of what "soon" does mean

It means that imminently you'll start taking steps towards your dreams.

For your dreams were given to you as your ongoing road map

Not as something unattainable --you're NOT headed for a
disappointment trap!

Instead your signs have given you glimpses of your future to keep
you going,

So please continue on in faith and with your seed-sowing.

For seeds are necessary in order for big trees to grow

That's you -- growing in faith and strength in all you know

"You know what you know" is key for you to remember now

As we turn the corner of Manifestation Street -- oh wow!

You're almost there -- it is all so very clear

DO NOT GIVE UP NOW, IT IS ALL SO VERY NEAR!

You'll be whisked there any time now with ease

So keep believing...please, please, please!

The Rose: How it Started My Sign Journey

Little did my friend Kathy know that she started me on the path towards living a life full of personal symbolism when she presented me with a rose bush in 1993. At the time, I was pregnant with my first child and was having a challenging pregnancy. At 20 weeks, I had to stop commuting into New York since I was already at risk due to too much exertion. Then, at 27 weeks, I had preterm labor and was rushed to the ER. Preterm labor can be dangerous, and may lead to premature birth, which results in greater health issues for your baby.

The doctor was able to give me meds that quieted down the labor, so I was able to go home, but then at 28 weeks I was once again too active and had to go to the ER, due to more preterm labor. I agreed to bed rest for the next 10 weeks of my pregnancy, due to my fear of having my baby almost three months too early.

That was when Kathy and St. Therese stepped in. Kathy and I believe in the tradition of saints. (Note: the rest of this book will NOT be focused on saints or a particular religion. Instead it will discuss personal signs that have meaning on an individual basis, whatever your beliefs may be.)

One day while I was on bed rest, Kathy brought a rose bush that she proceeded to plant in my garden. She then told me stories about St. Therese, also called the Little Flower. St. Therese of Lisieux lived from 1873-1897 in France, and was the youngest person ever to become a nun. She spent her life praying, philosophizing and teaching others her "little way" of kindness. Once she wrote that after she died, she would "spend time on earth doing good." One of the ways St. Therese promised to do good on earth was by providing a "shower of roses" to those who follow her path of kindness and who pray to her in good faith. Because of this, she is always depicted with a bouquet of roses in her arms. With her gift, Kathy jump-started my journey into

3

personal symbolism by giving me the rose bush in honor of my yet unborn child. During my long weeks on bedrest, I learned more about St. Therese and prayed to her daily for the health of my baby.

My prayers were answered since my daughter was born only 10 days early, instead of the original 10 to 12 weeks early. In fact, my daughter Alex was born just a few days prior to the annual celebration of St. Therese's life on September 30. Today, Alex is a healthy, vital young woman who does St. Therese's work "doing good" on earth by devoting her life to nonprofit work.

But that was just the beginning. St. Therese made me a firm believer in signs on my daughter's Christening day. I had asked Kathy to be Alex's godmother, and the baptism was in late November. Here in the Northeast U.S., my garden was naturally dormant. However, the morning we took Alex out for her Christening ceremony and celebratory party, St. Therese had a sign for us. On the rose bush that Kathy gave us, there was a single, beautiful rose blooming just for Alex's special day! We couldn't believe it! We took a photo of Alex by the rose and I still have that very flower -- now dried -- today.

My rose symbol also played a big part in my seven-year decision as to whether to have another child. I was very nervous about getting pregnant again after the scare I had during my pregnancy with Alex. I often prayed about it, however it wasn't until I was 39 years old that I made a decision. At that time, I finally ASKED God/The Universe/Spirit to give me a sign affirming whether I should have another child and whether it would be a healthy pregnancy and birth. A few minutes after I asked for this sign, I had to go pick up my daughter from her school which was just a short drive from my house. On the way home, I got my sign in the form of a huge hand-painted, glittery poster of a beautiful rose propped up on the side of the dingy train tracks that I had passed just 15 minutes earlier on the way to school! I almost hit the car in front of me because I was in such disbelief that I had so quickly received my primary personal symbol at that time: a rose! That sealed the deal for us regarding whether to try to become pregnant again. I was soon blessed with a carefree pregnancy and with the full-term, healthy birth of my son Ethan.

From the moment that I received the rose sign regarding my youngest child, the personal symbols started multiplying. There are now an abundance of signs of affirmation that I constantly see. The following chapters will weave in stories of how following those personal symbols gave me a virtual road map of affirmation to help me take positive, life-changing steps toward fulfillment. More importantly, it will also provide you with guidance and will help you achieve empowerment and happiness in your personal and professional life.

YOUR TAKEAWAY

How to decide what *your* signs are?

Repetition

As an English teacher, I am constantly telling my students that repetition in literature means that something important is being said. It is the author's way of telling the reader, "Pay attention!"

Similarly, when it comes to deciding what your personal symbols are, you need to start paying attention to details around you. Is there an object, name, number or song that keeps appearing in your life? If so, chances are that *you* should be paying attention..

Quantity

Is it uncanny that you are seeing a lot of this sign at once? It is probably NOT a coincidence, but instead it is a sign for you to be alert.

For example, a woman recently told me that the night after her beloved husband passed, she and her friends could not get over the fact that there were beetles in each room of her house. There were even rows of beetles on her walls! She then researched what beetles symbolize, and found that they represent immortality and renewal. Immediately, she knew it was a positive sign from her husband, and this comforted her, knowing that he was at peace and sending her a message of self-renewal.

Look up what the sign might mean

There are many resources online that can provide insight on what a sign might mean. Communities, like my larger brand "No Coincidences" platforms on Twitter, Instagram and Facebook, are open to your questions about your own signs. Our team can provide guidance.

While most signs and symbols have meanings, sometimes a sign is hard to decipher at first. That is okay. The mere fact that it keeps reappearing is good enough to start, since it will act as a compass going forward. You may want to try searching the symbolism of specific signs to point you in the right direction.

What has special meaning to you?

Roses started to have meaning to me since my friend Kathy gave me a rose bush during my high-risk pregnancy. Follow my lead, and ask yourself if there is something in your belief system that means a lot to you that might become a sign. Or perhaps there are certain affiliations of yours (college, favorite sports logos, etc.) that keep showing up in unexpected places; they too could be personal symbols. Or maybe something stands out because it is *not* familiar-- an unusual bird or animal, for instance, could be a sign.

Is it an unusual spot for that sign to appear ?

If this is the case, you can rest assured it is a personal symbol for you to follow. As mentioned, I saw a hand-painted poster of a rose propped up under a utility train track by my house, and knew that its appearance was so unusual that it had to be a sign.

Does a song or musical group come on often when you are thinking of someone close to you who passed?

I had a friend who loved the band Chicago, so whenever a song by Chicago comes on the radio, I know she is sending me a sign from beyond this life.

While my father was unusually open-minded toward rock music for someone born in 1927, he never really listened to Pink Floyd. However, for months, when I'd be in my car thinking about my deceased dad, a Pink Floyd song came on the radio. Thus, I now know that when I hear a Pink Floyd song -- especially *Wish You Were Here* -- that my dad is sending me a big hug, as well as affirmation that I am on the right path.

If someone you were close with passed away, they might be sending you signs. What did you often talk to them about? What educational, career affiliations did they have? What did they love? Any of those answers might end up being one of your personal symbols, and a way for them to "stay in touch."

CHAPTER 2

THE BUTTERFLY TAKES FLIGHT

Butterflies: What Does This Sign Mean?

Butterflies symbolize metamorphosis, as they transform from a caterpillar to a beautiful creature of flight who dazzles all as she flies. In particular, blue butterflies symbolize change in luck. Additionally, one species of blue butterflies, morpho butterflies, almost went extinct until one of the prominent conservation societies in the United States took great strides to repopulate them. In this chapter, you will see how I felt akin to these transformative blue butterflies as a personal symbol, since I too went from feeling almost lifeless inside to being filled with strength and grace, just like a blue butterfly.

Trust is a Must

Luisa Frey

You're seeking -- but what have you found?
Shh….listen…I hear a sound

The sound of you yearning to move forwards with grace and ease
Not to go back to that which did not fully please.

Your soul so seeks an outlet in which to express itself
To center, breathe, and to shift away from "lack" when it comes to wealth.

There is no door holding you back from achieving a state of Zen
For if you don't learn to trust your signs now -- then when?

For life will continue at its galloping pace
Until you stop, listen and face…

Face the other direction -- as in, not reaching for the past.
Instead, reach for the future – that which will grow roots and last.

It's there for the taking, only you hold the key
To open the door filled with joyous things that you did not foresee!

My two proverbial "roses," my daughter and son, continued to grow and bloom beautifully, but my marriage did not. After months of counseling and asking for signs, my then-husband and I took the big, scary step of separation and divorce. There were so many things to be concerned about: first and foremost was my children's wellbeing, followed by my lack of financial security, and how to keep up and care for my big, old house.

Needless to say, these were tremendously difficult and emotional times. They took their toll on me emotionally and physically with many a night tossing and turning at 3 a.m. as I wondered how I would be able to pay my bills, afford health insurance, and swing a college education for my daughter and son.

During the wee hours of the morning when I could not sleep, I started writing down in my journal the "three good things" that happened the day before. There were times I really felt like I was grasping at straws -- my life sucked at that time, as it was filled with grief for my disintegrated marriage, stress over my lack of financial stability and a whole lot of loneliness. However, my belief in signs helped me find "three good things" to write about daily. For example, cardinals would often appear in my life -- be it the real bird or through images or objects -- and I would record the cardinal signs in my journals as one of the "three good things." It is important to note that female cardinals represent following your intuition and male cardinals represent perseverance, as in, better days are ahead. These particular personal symbols kept me going for quite a while.

What made this time even more distressing was that I had been self-employed for the past 15 years as a family travel writer, and therefore had to take on an enormous amount of financial pressure once I got divorced. As you can guess, having your own business does not always ensure you will have a regular paycheck. Additionally, I now had to pay for an individual health insurance plan, which was prohibitive. I was not equipped with financial know-how, and realized that I needed a better financial plan ASAP.

In an effort to increase my income, I morphed my travel writing business to encompass family travel marketing as well. The linchpin of the business was a newly created blog called Teen Travel Talk, written by and for teenagers so that they would feel more included in family travel conversations. I worked extremely hard to grow the blog and its following; also, I marketed my social media, writing and marketing services to travel companies that wanted more of the family market. This was an extremely labor-intensive process since I was now responsible for monthly payroll since I had hired a number of young adults to serve as content creators. In addition to my social media learning curve, I also had no financial background, as my former husband had taken care of everything related to our finances. I lacked the confidence to take charge of my finances right away, but I sought out helpful people along the way to assist me in those aspects of my business and personal life.

As I became more confident in my abilities to deal with business and personal finances, I noticed that my friends started to unknowingly give me presents that had blue butterflies on them. I then supplemented this plethora of butterfly objects by buying two huge, blue butterfly wings from the Halloween store, which I hung over my bed, along with dozens of other butterfly presents, ranging from plaques to butterfly stained glass pieces. Of course, butterflies -- especially blue butterflies -- then became one of my signs to guide me along the way.

The Gift of the Blue Butterfly

Luisa Frey

Roses are red, roses are blue

And lest you doubt it, butterflies are blue too!

Rebirth is what blue butterflies stand for

As in spreading one's wings and so much more.

What, you might ask, does a blue butterfly mean?

It represents obtaining the impossible, believing in the unseen.

And that is what following the signs mean to me,

For they give confirmation of that which only I can see.

YOUR TAKEAWAY:

Your Thoughts Count!

YOU are the most important part of the process of learning how to interpret your personal symbols. Below are questions for you to consider and answer; doing so will help you learn how to identify and to process the signs you regularly see and hear.

1. What are the numbers in your birthday or in your family members' birthdays?

_____

_____

2. What other numbers have significance to you? This could be an anniversary or other special day.

_____

_____

3. Is there an animal, insect or bird that you see often, even though it is unusual for you to see it in that place? (For example, I live in a congested area

14

of NJ and so the time I saw a fox in my neighborhood, it was unusual and therefore a sign to me.). Write it here.

_____

_____

4. What songs do you associate with:

4a. Happy times

_____

_____

4b. Times of accomplishment

_____

_____

4c. Letting go of the past

_____

_____

4d. Someone you were close with who has passed away

_____

_____

5. Is there a holy person, prophet or someone of note in your belief system that you feel drawn to?

_____

_____

5a. If so, what is his/her name?

_____

_____

5b. Research and write the significance of that person here.

_____

_____

6. Are there any key phrases from a poem or a saying that means a lot to you? If so, write them here.

_____

_____

7. What else has meaning to you?

_____

_____

7a. What is the physical representation of that?

_____

_____

Review this list periodically to see if you are hearing or seeing any of these on a regular basis. Ask yourself: What was happening at that time? What were you thinking?

These personal symbols can be a way of affirming your thoughts and actions at the time they appeared.

CHAPTER 3

THE GREAT BLUE HERON PATIENTLY WAITS

Great Blue Heron: What Does This Sign Mean?

Great blue herons are majestic birds -- if you've ever seen one fly you will never forget it due to their delicate yet wide wingspan. However, when you see them wading in water waiting to catch the next fish that swims by, it is hard to believe they are so powerful since they possess very skinny, long legs. What is most remarkable about herons is that they are very patient and wait for the right time to make their move to catch their next meal. This is where blue herons gain their symbolism since, as a sign, herons mean being patient -- yet not giving up hope and trust -- and making a move once the right opportunity comes along. So often I have seen blue herons wait and wait and then, of course, with a swift move, they grab their intended goal (aka, dinner)!

During this trying post-divorce time of getting on my feet emotionally and financially, my dad Frank died. I felt abandoned, alone, scared and sad. Also, a month after my divorce, I was scared that I might have ovarian cancer. Thankfully, the growth in my ovary was benign. The three in a row gut punch -- divorce, my dad's passing, and a health scare -- really tested my faith. So often in my journals I wrote: "My life sucks! When is it going to get better?" However, as I have found, the times of greatest darkness can open the door to growth and new direction.

Soon after my dad's passing, I started seeing a great blue heron in the park in town. It's unusual to see such large and unique waterfowl in my town since we live only 11 miles from New York City. Due to the reoccurrence of seeing the blue heron at various spots in my town's extensive park system, I knew it must be a sign sent from my dad.

Indeed, the symbolic meaning of this bird was very applicable to me at the time. Because of this sign, I knew then that I had to keep searching for my path to financial security while being patient at the same time. Most importantly, I knew that eventually my patience, hard work, intelligence and openness to the signs would result in financial security and abundance -- even though the sky seemed quite dark at the time.

Winds of Change Poem
Luisa Frey

Listen closely to your soul to hear its guidance and its glow

For where you'll be led, only the Divine truly knows

And that's why you need to stay in the light

For when it comes to signs, do not be scared and take flight

Just keep giving it up to the Universe -- try as hard as you can

Because it's unfolding beautifully, according to an ultimate plan.

Understanding how signs and personal symbolism might occur

So you may be starting to dip your toe into trusting the guidance that signs are giving you along the way. However, since we are all inquisitive humans, you may be asking yourself, "Ok, but how does that sign seem to magically appear just in time for me to see it?"

The answer is Divine orchestration. This is when a sign or helpful person, often identified by others as a coincidence, appears in your path. Often it is so remarkable that it can be seen as a sign of Divine orchestration, whereby only a power as mighty as the Universe could have orchestrated all the players to be in place just in time for you to see that sign or to meet that helpful person. Divine orchestration is often seen by some as an answer to a prayer.

YOUR TAKEAWAY

Tips for Seeing and Receiving Signs and Personal Symbols

Get quiet

My mother would always say, "How come signs come to you and not to me?" My response was "Actually, signs come to everyone. You just need to get quiet in order to notice them."

One of the prime ways I do this is to meditate. I've been meditating daily for 34 years and this quietness has made me more in tune with signs and my intuition. If you find meditating difficult, then try it with an online guided meditation recording or relaxation music in the background.

Other ways to get quiet in order to see and be open to signs is to do yoga regularly. At the end of most yoga classes, participants are led on a guided visualization exercise which is similar to meditation. If neither meditation or yoga are for you, then try getting unplugged regularly and going for walks alone outside. You will be amazed at the unspoken signs you see along the way!

Journaling

Record your signs in a journal at night or the next morning. Date these entries, jot down what is happening in your life at the time, as well as write about your hopes and dreams. I have written in over 50 journals over a period of nine years! These journals have not only been a reference for me to review and see how the signs are guiding me, but they lift me up whenever I write in them. Journals are a place to put your thoughts and emotions; once I do this, I am ready to face my day in a very positive way.

Take photos of the signs

When possible, try to take a photo of the sign you are seeing. Once you practice seeing signs regularly, they appear more frequently. I need to take photos of them on my phone in order to remember what they were when I sit down to record them in my journal.

Awareness

This is perhaps the simplest one to do -- take a deep breath and become aware of your surroundings. Don't we often run through life from one thing to another and never realize the simple beauty and synchronicities that are around us?

Ask for a sign

Don't be afraid to ask the Universe to bring you a sign. Once you do, then let it go and go about your normal business. You will be amazed at the signs you receive!

Expect magical things to occur...and they will!

Worthy of Receiving
Luisa Frey

The time has come for all good men and women to shine
Have no doubt, this poem has been sent from the Divine

For Divinely given is how all your signs are always sent
Because the Universe knows you understand what all these signs
have meant.

While your life right now seems so far from the ideal,
Trust your signs and how they make you truly feel.

You've listened, trusted and taken guided action so many times
Especially due to all your many encouraging signs.

You are now opening the door to your new life filled with
manifestation and ease
Soon you'll be filled with endless "thank yous" instead of "please"

You should be so proud of all that you've learned and how you've
grown
Now it's all visibly blooming -- all the seeds that you've sown...

Seeds of abundance, joy, laughter -- there's no more wait

...for true manifestation. Get ready, it's almost time to celebrate!

CHAPTER 4

HELPFUL PEOPLE & NUMBERS AS SIGNS

Keep the Faith

Luisa Frey

You are a little bird ready for glorious flight
But instead, you're focusing on the fright.

There is nothing to fear in your tomorrow
Please hand the Universe each and every sorrow.

For then you will be brought quickly back to the light
Don't feel you have to continually try with all your might

Instead, there is so much potential for you to transfigure

So close your eyes, take a deep breath and voila -- it is all configured.

Remember to put it all into the Universe's hands

And it will lead you to happiness in the Promised Land.

Helpful People Along the Way

When I put my mind to something, I give it 200% and I do not give up easily. When the financial aspects of my business were not moving forward as quickly as I had anticipated, I just kept working harder and harder. While that is generally an attribute, in hindsight I now see it as one of the reasons why I stayed with my family travel marketing business perhaps longer than I should have. There was a lot of money I had to invest to keep the teen travel blog going, and there was even more time I had to devote to pitching potential marketing clients. I ended up accruing debt since I invested in my business for quite a while and I thought it would pay off big time in the end.

Often, when I was despairing over a rejection from a company that I had, in vain, attempted to get as a client, one of my sibling's high school acquaintances, Jack, would pop up in public spaces in our town. This generally occurred randomly, such as when I was either walking in the park or driving around town doing errands. I'd usually be at the breaking point in my life but then I'd see Jack. Sometimes it was in passing without any words exchanged. Therefore, seeing him was just a sign to keep the faith. Other times I'd see him while I was walking in the park. Upon these occasions, he'd often offer words of spiritual guidance to help keep me open to where the proverbial path was leading me.

Finally, 3-1/2 years after the inception of my blog, I realized that I just could not keep doing things the same way. The financial stress was over the top. Plus, I was tired of working alone -- I longed for the company of others during the work day. While I did have some clients, they were not enough to pay for my overhead AND leave me and my children enough to live on.

Since I was a big reader of spiritual books, I knew that sometimes things don't work out because that is not where we are meant to be at that time. This was a hard pill to swallow since my blog and my business had become "my baby" that I had created, nurtured, and grew. And so, with a heavy heart, in January 2013, I started to look for a full-time writing job with benefits in corporate America. This was NOT what I really wanted to do but I felt I had to pursue this avenue for the sake of my kids and my mental health. I felt defeated and that I was waving the white flag.

White flags symbolize surrender, such as when a foe succumbs to the conqueror; at the time, I felt the shame that waving a white flag connotes. However, in hindsight I see that I needed to indeed "surrender" to what the Universe had planned for me. I had to trust in my signs more than ever before in order to help give me direction and solace.

Soon after, I got up the courage to announce to friends that I was giving up my business and instead seeking a corporate writing job in NYC. A friend, who had been an informal business mentor, reached out to me via email. His email, and Jack's random appearances, are prime examples of how helpful people, who pop into your life, can be a form of a sign too. They can point you in a direction or help you see why the path you have been on might not be the right one at this point.

Here's what his email said after I advised him I was giving up my business in order to seek a corporate writing job:

"I don't want to say I'm sorry to hear that because I feel like you gave it your all, learned a lot and grew. These are all good things and things that you will take with you to your next endeavor. And maybe after striking out on your own, you're a little braver. Maybe now that you did it, maybe it will be easier to be bold in the future and take more chances. I know you have had to make many difficult decisions these last few years and it's been very hard at times. I have a great deal of respect for that and I am proud of you. Keep me posted on your progress and good luck!"

And that, indeed, is a prime example of how helpful people can pop into your life when you need the courage most.

Helpful friends along the way...
point the way to a new career

Soon after I decided to curtail my family travel marketing business, I ran into Jack a few more times. This time it was in the waiting room at a doctor's office so we had time to chat. Each time I'd see him, he'd suggest I go to a Quaker Meeting House service since he knew that I had been meditating daily for over 30 years. Quaker services are held in silence so that attendees can meditate for close to an hour. It seemed like a good fit for me, so that spring I started attending the nearby Quaker Meeting House about twice a month. I relished the silence and presence of those who are known pacifists. Little did I know that it would lead me to a new career, but not the one I had expected. Instead, a helpful person from the Quaker Meeting House pointed me in the direction of a new career that is now quite near and dear to my heart and has given me the financial security and personal fulfillment that I was seeking.

YOUR TAKEAWAY

How Helpful People can be Signs

How do you know when friends and helpful people are saying something to you that can be interpreted as a directional road sign for you? First, think about what a friend -- or sometimes even a stranger -- said to you when you were at the crossroads in your life. It may not often be what you want to hear but instead what you need to hear.

For example, while I knew who Jack was, he was not someone I'd automatically think of going to for advice. However, I was observant and noticed that Jack seemed to appear right when I was going through major challenges in my life. As a result, I felt that it was no coincidence each time I ran into him. I listened to his wisdom because it felt like it was a sign pointing me in the right direction -- and it was.

Blessed by Friends
Luisa Frey

I've often thought, "what is a friend?"
It's someone who's there for you, beginning to end.

Someone who's willing to take your hand and lead
Especially during your times of need.

When I look back at this past year
Naturally I could shed many a tear

But what I'd rather focus on is how blessed I have been
To have had a friend like you stick by me through thick and thin!

CHAPTER 5

DIVINE ORCHESTRATION &

NUMBERS OF AFFIRMATION

Numbers: What do numbers as signs mean?

Numerology is the study of the meaning of specific numbers. It interprets numbers as a way that the Universe sends the receiver (you) messages through those numbers. The numbers one through nine each have a specific meaning and thus they are the building blocks for interpretation of more complex numerals.

While I am not an expert on numerology, I do know that within numerology there are three numbers called master numbers: 11, 22, 33 which have extra special meaning. Some people believe that Jesus died when he was 33 years old and so, in some circles, this is why 33 is believed to be a master number; additionally, 11 and 22 obviously add up to 33 which also makes it a spiritual number. Also, when one is seeing double, repeating numbers, for example 1122 or 922 or 444, it can be interpreted as a big sign of affirmation for whatever you are thinking or contemplating. In effect, it is like a green light saying, "GO!"

However, there may be certain numbers that are not double numbers but may have meaning to you such as a loved one's birthdate or any other number of significances. For example, my friend Gail's "sign number," which serves as an affirmation for her, is her late mother's favorite number of 18 since it is a spiritual number in Judaism and stands for "chai" (life). Or maybe you keep waking up – without an alarm clock – at a specific time each day. The numbers of that time might represent a sign, so look up what they symbolically mean.

For me, the number 11 was my number of affirmation for a short period of time when I first started my journey into the meaning of signs. For example, I'd often just happen to look at the clock and it was 11:11. I then "graduated" into the next master number, 22, as my number of affirmation. This number has had HUGE significance in my life and has guided me many times when I had to make a big decision but was not 100% sure what I should do. In these situations, I kept seeing the 22 in so many unusual places and situations that I then became quite sure I was making the right decision and indeed taking the correct big steps forward.

Destined

Luisa Frey

You are beautiful, you are wise
You are destined to an amazingly beautiful surprise

Dry your tears, pat your wet eyes
For here comes the best surprise

It's beautiful, it's gorgeous, just like you
And it'll help you stop questioning all you do

It's here, it's imminently falling in your lap
And it'll make others stand up for you and clap

Clap and cheer and say "Wow, what a gal, who is ever so strong"
Just keep the faith a few minutes more, for it won't be long...

...It won't be long until you sing Jerusalem's song, like the days of
yore
The song of abundance and riches -- gone are the days of feeling
poor.

Go now, lift yourself back to the light as you always do

For the best gift yet is imminently coming to you!

Divine Orchestration of Helpful People & Numbers of Affirmation

As mentioned in the previous chapter, I started applying for writing jobs in NYC as I was planning to give up my family travel marketing business. However, on three occasions I was the second finalist choice I interviewed for and most of these jobs had applicant pools of about 400 to 500 people. However, being second choice does NOT land you a job nor pay the bills. I was starting to despair. I was also starting to wonder why I got so close on three occasions but I did not get these jobs in the end. Perhaps a writing gig in NYC was NOT where I was supposed to be?

As previously mentioned, to keep my spirits up, I took the advice of my acquaintance Jack who suggested that I attend the Quaker Meeting House to meditate and find peace. After attending the Quaker Meeting House a few times, I met a man named Mike who was also from the town where I live. We started talking after the meetings and eventually met for coffee. Mike had been a lawyer but mid-life he made a big career change and became a high school economics and political science teacher. He did this by getting certified via the Alternate Route Program, which is not available in all states but is in the state of New Jersey where I live. Mike was quite fulfilled in his new teaching career.

Early that summer, Mike and I were planning on getting together for dinner, however, things got too busy with us, both due to summer vacations. So we made a long-range date to meet in August after our respective vacations. In hindsight, it is a good thing we met before the new school year started.

The Stage is Set
Luisa Frey

The stage is set and the glory is about to begin
Told you that your life would turn out "win, win, win."

All the doors are now open up so very wide
And you've opened YOUR arms and welcomed abundance inside

For "joyful" will soon be a part of your name
And from today on, your life will never be the same.

Gone are the days of worry, fear and sadness
Yeeha! The horizon is full of untold gladness

For your ship has set sail for the Isle of Unbelievable Mirth
Which has been here for the taking, since your birth.

You'll continue to be sent signs and people to help hold your hand
As you are so very close to reaching the Promised Land.

Go now in faith and also in pure love
For this covenant has been sealed at the Sign of the Dove.

The Excitement and Number Signs are Building

Fast forward to the period between early July, when Mike and I set a date to get together later that summer, and August when we finally met for dinner. During this time, the amount of signs and positive messages I was receiving when I meditated and journaled was off the charts! Repeatedly after meditating, I'd write in my journal, "I have a feeling that BIG, positive things are coming to me!" Another day, I wrote in my journal, "My light is shining very strongly now. Do NOT doubt the signs and energy I'm feeling about colossal, positive change in my life! Do NOT doubt that my ship has indeed come in! I am positively manifesting and attracting money, fulfillment and joy." I even decluttered my office in order to make room for the new, which I felt was on its way.

Then, the #22 signs started coming fast and furiously. It is interesting to note that I attended Boston College during the Doug Flutie years and his jersey number was, you guessed it, #22. In fact, I associate Flutie with my dad since we joyously saw Flutie's famous Hail Mary pass together, and I will never forget the shared joy my dad and I experienced at that moment! So, in effect, my dad guides me through many signs, be it the great blue heron, which began appearing to me after my father's passing, the number 22 and more.

Speaking of Boston, the following happened all in one day while I was visiting Boston during this time frame. I received a hotel statement saying I had 22,000 frequent visitor points accrued; a friend texted me that she owed me $22; the public bathroom at Boston College's student center was room #122; the Fenway Park tickets to see Paul McCartney in concert were in section #22; I saw a blue butterfly sign at 7:22; the cab we took after the concert was #4222; and a magazine I looked at in the hotel said 22nd Annual Awards. As my dear friend

Dr. John has often said when I tell him stories about my signs, "You can't make this stuff up!" I filled so many journal pages during this month-long period in which the signs were over the top. I KNEW that something big and beautiful was about to occur. I just wasn't sure what the big, beautiful thing was!

It was still two more weeks until Mike and I were going to meet for dinner and continually, I filled my journals with messages that came to me when I was meditating. One, from July 11, said, "Trust yourself, trust your signs...Wow -- what's going to manifest? Such incredible excitement is felt around me!" A few days later I wrote, "My life has come full circle now. Keep trusting that the time has come to make major life changes that are full of positive shifts. Trust is a must! All these mega signs are here to keep me in faith. It is coming to me now!" But, I wondered, WHAT IS IT???

Then I started waking up at 4:44 a.m. for many days in a row. Each time I'd wake up so early, I'd toss and turn; finally I'd get up to meditate and journal to relax my mind and body. Often these journal entries would state, "Do NOT doubt the big, positive changes happening now that I can feel. The abundance I seek is manifesting now so that I will see it imminently. It is coming with ease! Trust, trust, trust the signs and helpful people!"

Then two days before I had dinner with Mike, I wrote in my journal, "Big, beautiful things are coming to me NOW!" Hmmm....but what could that be? And the day before our dinner, I wrote in my journal, "I have a feeling that my life is about to take an abrupt turn down positive manifestation lane." I then drew a stick figure at a crossroads of two roads with a sharp turn right ahead -- and a smile on the face of the stick figure.

Finally, on August 11, about a month after we first spoke about getting together and after hundreds of signs and messages filling my journal that big, positive things are imminent, I had dinner with Mike. It was a pleasant night filled with enlightening conversation. During our chat, I told Mike about the fifteen years I volunteered as co-president of our town's Academic Booster Club. I shared my passion for hands-on learning and detailed the many successful "edu-taining" programs I started in our school district.

Upon hearing about my passion for educating youngsters, Mike started to tell me about his journey to becoming a high school teacher via New Jersey's Alternate Route Program. Mike then said, "Why don't you go back to school and simultaneously do the Alternate Route Program to become a high school English teacher?" Talk about an "aha moment!" It was as if God had whispered in his ear to say this to me!

I replied, "Why didn't I think of that before?" My mom was a high school English teacher. She was so well loved by her students and she really made a difference in so many lives. That night after Mike left, I wrote in my journal, "Aha! Mike gave me a great idea that feels right - - I think that I'm going to pursue it!" By the time I woke up the next morning, he had sent me links to the New Jersey Department of Education's Alternate Route Program website. I was off and running!

Manifestation Does Now Start for a Big & Healed Heart

Luisa Frey

You are beautiful, you are wise
You are in for a delightful surprise!

The wait is over, the time is here
For amazingly beautiful to manifest for you, so dear!

Really, truly, it is happening now and any day you will see
All the awesome manifestations that lovingly await thee

Financial security? Check, that one's in the bag
No more cash will you lag

Get ready, since the train pulling in the station is one of positive manifestation
So get on your dancing shoes for a multi-day celebration!

You finally feel confident and that makes a world of difference now
There's so much excitement that you keep saying "oh wow!"

"Oh wow, the signs I heard, saw and wrote have all come to beautiful fruition"

And yep, even there's now a way to finance your kids' college tuition.

Go now, without a care in the your big 'n healed heart

For right now, positive manifestation does truly start!

YOUR TAKEAWAY

Tips for Interpreting the Meaning of Signs

Look up the meaning online

While others' interpretation of signs may not always fit your circumstances, I have still found them to be a helpful jumping off point for my own interpretation. Online searches using the key words such as "meaning of…" or "symbolism of …" are great ways to start.

Pinpoint when you saw the sign

What were you going through or thinking about when you saw that sign? Keep track of that because chances are that the sign will be an answer to that thought or situation.

Go to your religion for guidance

Whatever your beliefs, there may be some type of positive correlation to that sign. As previously mentioned, I kept seeing roses as one of my signs which in turn connected to St. Therese and her messages of faith.

Write it down

In your journal, write down what you think the sign might mean. It might change in time, however, it may not.

Additional advice

Get images of your signs and display them around your home and office. These serve as positive reminders of the things that your signs symbolize to you.

YOUR THOUGHTS COUNT!

YOU are the most important part of the process of learning how to interpret signs. Below are some more questions for you to answer; by doing so it will help you learn how to process the signs you are seeing and hearing.

By figuring out how you remember and process information the most, it will help you go through the interpretation process when you come across signs. That way you can remember and discern those signs later when you are in a quiet place.

1. How do you remember things the most? Number the below in order of how you remember things easily. (#1 is the most; #4 is the least)

a. Hearing

_____

_____

b. Seeing/Reading

_____

_____

c. Writing things down

_____

_____

d. Taking a photo of the object or situation

_____

_____

e. Other

_____

_____

2. What way feels most comfortable regarding recording your signs?
(#1 is the most; #4 is the least)

a. Journal

_____

_____

b. Taking a photo

_____

_____

c. Verbally recording them on your phone

_____

_____

3. Based on your #1 and #2 choices above, consider utilizing those modalities for recording your personal symbols.

CHAPTER 6

EIFFEL TOWER

Eiffel & His Tower: What Does This Sign Mean?

When Gustave Eiffel's plans for his tower won the competition for the 1889 World's Fair in Paris, there were a multitude of naysayers. People were concerned that it would not be safe, that his mathematical calculations might not be feasible and that it would be an eyesore compared to Notre Dame and Arc de Triomphe. It took 300 men three years to build Eiffel Tower and it only had a 20-year lease. It was almost demolished after 20 years but was spared. Thank goodness since today it is one of the most iconic and most popular attractions in the world.

I started seeing a lot of Eiffel Tower signs right around the time that I was taking my big steps to go back to school to become an English teacher. After researching the Eiffel Tower a bit, I learned that Gustave Eiffel kept his faith and vision despite the seemingly adverse forces around him. Thus, I took my Eiffel Tower signs to mean "keep going -- trust yourself." After mentioning this to friends, they often gave me mini replicas of Eiffel Towers and all kinds of items with

Eiffel Tower logos on them. Now I have a collection of Eiffel Towers in my living room and dining room!

Manifestation Day
Luisa Frey

Your beautiful life is right outside your door
Time to open it wide -- here comes more and more

Look at the sunshine, bask in the breeze
It's all manifesting now -- with EASE!

You are easing your heart by saying what you need and deserve
You're taking so many brave steps where others wouldn't have the nerve

"Woohoo!" will be your new phrase of exclamation
Voiced again and again -- it's all part of your celebration.

The invitations have been sent out to all who've helped you along the way
Your big fiesta is going to happen now and any day

For your treasure indeed was always at the end of the rainbow
Soon all will hear how you listened and trusted what you know

This is truly what the past few years have been about for you
To give up your fears and NOT worry about the how's and the who

For you are about to be given the biggest bouquet of roses you've ever seen

Any day now, when it happens, you'll know what this means!

Keep telling your story about how you kept inching out on the limb and saying "yes"

And because of that trust and courage, it's all turning out better than the best!

Luisa and her Tower

Needless to say, when I threw my hat quite rapidly into the ring and started chasing all the criteria needed to get my Alternate Route Teaching Certification, I saw Eiffel Tower signs in quite an abundance. Keep in mind that the thunderbolt idea to get my teaching certification came about two to three weeks before colleges started their fall semesters, so I had to make a game plan ASAP. The NJ Department of Education's (NJDOE) Alternate Route website was confusing and the many hurdles that I needed to complete were daunting, to say the least.

My first step was to enroll in a NJDOE 24-hour, pre-teaching class. Upon inquiry, the class "just so happened" to be offered the next week at a nearby NJ state university and there "just so happened" to be space in this class. This was the first of so many things that fell into place quickly so that these synchronicities -- coupled with my constant signs -- helped me trust that this scary, big step was meant to be.

My journal entry on August 19, 2013, was: "I'm so excited -- I'm going to my first of the 24-hours of pre-teaching classes offered by the state. Yay -- feels good!" Upon getting to the class, we had to do group work. I had on my Eiffel Tower earrings and noticed that my sign was being reflected back at me since one of the women in my group also was wearing Eiffel Tower earrings. This was followed by the teacher mentioning Paris twice in her morning lecture as well as an image of the Eiffel Tower on the television when I got home. The repetitive Eiffel Tower signs were affirming that I wouldn't fall during my leap of faith.

Upon completion of the 24-hour course that Friday, August 23, my journal entry stated: "After I was meditating today, I wrote that I have 'taken an abrupt turn down manifestation street and that doors to financial security, joy and love will continue to open quickly' for me" -

- and they did! The Eiffel Tower signs continued to be in abundance since, a few days later, I was exploring a town in Connecticut and stumbled across a gourmet chocolate store. Upon entering, there was a huge box of chocolates with -- you guessed it -- an Eiffel Tower logo on it. The following day my son got a postcard from his good friend who was on vacation. I bet you can by now figure out what was the picture on the postcard -- yup, the Eiffel Tower. These were great signs to help keep me moving forward quickly. The next day I called my alma mater, Boston College, to get my four year transcript needed for the NJ Department of Education (NJDOE) to calculate how many English classes I still needed in order to teach high school. Thus, I was ready to explore which colleges I could quickly matriculate for graduate, non-degree courses needed to fulfill requirements for teaching high school English.

However, I was super concerned about how I would financially swing not only my tuition, but also my daughter's college tuition and everyday expenses during the year – or more – that I might have to be at school. It was going to be a while until NJDOE reviewed my transcript and advised me which Boston College journalism and English classes would go towards my teaching certification. Thus, I was unsure if I could even complete this whole process by May so that I could be teaching by September. Financially, though, I could not go out on a limb longer than a year.

This seemed Herculean but the signs as well as the affirmations I got during meditation kept me in a place of positivity rather than fear. On August 29, I recorded in my journal, "I just turned on House Hunters International on television and guess where they were? Paris, of course!" These signs helped me take the next step which was to again call Boston College to try to get a syllabi describing my English and journalism courses to aid NJDOE in deciding whether they'd go towards my needed 30 credits of English. Without this knowledge, I had no idea how many credits I needed for teaching certification. Yet another synchronicity occurred when I made that call since the person I spoke with at BC said, "You're in luck! Just last week we got all our past course syllabi archived!" This was exactly what I needed to send NJDOE for their review of my college credits.

You Can't Make this Stuff Up!

All my focus now was to see which college in my area would matriculate me asap and which would make the most sense for me to attend in order to get additional English credits needed for certification. I spent a number of days making inquiries and talking to my friends and mentors, including Barbara. Formerly the head of Special Services in my town and a colleague of my mom-the-English-teacher, Barbara was very generous with her time to help me find a path to make this happen.

After getting my daughter Alex settled back at Boston College over Labor Day weekend, I knew that it was now or never regarding matriculation for classes that were beginning later that week. I called Montclair State University, which has a great teaching program, and got an appointment with the registrar's office. They reviewed my Boston College transcript and matriculated me immediately in the graduate school/non-degree program.

However, there was a huge sign awaiting me. The registrar said that the next step was to go to the assistant dean's office down the hall to make sure there were English classes available that would fit my needs before I paid the hefty semester fee. When I walked into the assistant dean's office, I was speechless and he could tell. He saw the look on my face and said, "Is everything ok?" I replied, "I know this sounds crazy but I have a thing about the symbolism of the Eiffel Tower and Paris. AND YOUR OFFICE IS COVERED WITH EIFFEL TOWER AND PARIS MEMENTOES!" As my friend Dr. John often said, you can't make this stuff up!

Of course, these signs totally affirmed that there was no turning back -- this was meant to be. Despite my huge financial concerns and fears about taking a year to complete my coursework and change careers, these signs affirmed that it would all work out. And indeed, the assistant dean had the level of classes I needed. I signed up, paid my tuition and ran out to get notebooks for classes that were starting in two days!

YOUR TAKEAWAY

Tips for Interpreting a String of Signs

Not only has my dear friend Dr. John often said to me, "You can't make this stuff up" when he was listening to my stories about the synchronicities of my signs, but he also remarked "you're getting an entire PARAGRAPH of signs!" And he's right. The more I was open to recording, interpreting and acting upon my signs, the more they came to me in a gushing flow. The end result is what one could categorize as a paragraph of information which really gave me profound and trusted guidance.

1. Start with an inner dialogue with the Universe

Don't forget to first ASK for a sign(s). When I first started on this journey, I would ask the Universe for a sign. However, the more I became aware of signs, the less I needed to ask for one -- instead, they just appeared in rapidity without me asking for them.

2. Journal and record the signs

Both of these practices help you decipher what the signs mean. So many times I'm in the midst of writing the signs down when I get an "ah ha" moment that helps me figure out what those signs might mean as a whole "paragraph."

3. Deciphering if it is a single sign or if there is a longer message involved

Often, when I am in the midst of a new endeavor or taking steps that are out of my comfort zone, I will see a sign. This can be interpreted as the green light signal for me to keep moving in that direction. However, sometimes I will see a string of signs that are seemingly unrelated to each other. Upon closer inspection I can piece them together and get some clarity on a situation -- as in a whole "paragraph."

4. Talk to friends about the signs

By doing so, they may say something that sparks that "ah ha" moment of interpretation for you.

YOUR WORDS WILL BE A
BALM FOR FAMILIES

This is an excerpt from a long, beautiful message I wrote down in meditation while listening to a choir singing medieval music in Notre Dame cathedral in Paris in May, 2011. I now see how prophetic it was regarding how my words -- as an English teacher for students with learning challenges -- create a balm for families. However when I recorded this guidance, I did not have teaching on my radar at all!

You are glorious in your light and energy now

And this light will act as a lightning rod

To attract amazingly beautiful things and people to you

You are glorious in your light and your work precedes you --

As in, you are encroaching on groundbreaking work

Your words will uncover mountains of positives for yourself and others

Your words will create a balm that will anoint families

Your words are strong -- like a voice in the wilderness

Yet they soothe, comfort, acknowledge and guide.

The dam is bursting open with riches you never even dreamed of

The door has opened and you are about to see the many presents being bestowed upon you.

CHAPTER 7

SONG SIGNS - PART 1

Don't Stop Believing & Let it Be

Song Signs: What Do These Signs Mean?

Many years ago on my sign journey, I realized that my car radio was my biggest facilitator of signs. So often I'd be in my car thinking about a situation and a song would come on that either: reminded me of my dad or a few close friends who had passed; was the exact answer to what I was pondering; or provided me with the lift-me-up I needed to keep the faith. In fact, my friends became aware of this and when my 14-year-old car died, they asked if there was a way to keep the "magic radio" despite selling the car! I told them that the magic is not in the radio, but in one's trust and interpretation of the song signs that one is receiving via the radio.

Sure enough, my new car has a "magic radio" too. This time, my car has Sirius so that the title of the song comes on the screen. Thus, if I am not driving when a sign song comes on, I'll take a picture of it on my phone. I flip through my photos as I'm sitting down to journal and then record these song signs. This is a great and easy way to keep track of the messages one is getting via song signs.

Do Not Fear

Luisa Frey

Do not fret, do not fear
For huge financial relief is almost here

Do NOT think so far ahead in fear
Because financial stability is almost here

While it may not look like that right now to you
It's coming to you swiftly -- like a rose of blue!

Blue roses symbolize reaching the unattainable, or so it appears
In this case, blue roses show that your financial relief is here

For you are where you are supposed to be
It's ALL in place, don't you see?

See the glory, the joy, the release, the sun
As you pay your bills, make sure you save time for fun!

It's all here and it's here now, that's for sure
The doors are open and you have walked through them for a cure

A cure of the "financial fear blues" -- phew, they're gone now

And all that's left is the exclamation, "oh wow!"

Oh wow, I did it and I've got it made in the shade
And the sun, the joy, the peace and fulfillment is never gonna fade.

DON'T STOP BELIEVING

From the moment I stepped onto Montclair State University's (MSU) campus, I knew that pursuing a career in education was the right move. I had always been an enthusiastic student and although it was 30 years since I had been in school, I felt right at home at MSU.

The first semester, I took two classes -- mind you, last time I was in school was during the dinosaur days (before computers and internet) so there was a lot to get used to. However, the song signs were kicking into place which affirmed the positive messages I was receiving in meditation about the new road I had taken. In fact, the night before I started my first class at MSU, "Don't Stop Believing" came on my car radio, which indeed became a very apt anthem for the next year.

Meanwhile, I was juggling two part time jobs in order to keep myself financially afloat. For my tuition, I had used up what little post-divorce savings I had and charged the rest. This certainly was a risky move and on September 6, I wrote in my journal, "please have money fall into my lap" and again and again, the signs kept affirming for me to keep moving forward. The next time I meditated I wrote the following message, "I am entering a manifestation zone where professional and financial matters are coming together quickly, easily and happily. Keep trusting the process. Keep trusting yourself. Keep trusting your signs." This was then followed by Pink Floyd's "Wish you were here" and again, "Don't Stop Believing." Although my dad, who passed four years earlier, was not a Pink Floyd fan, he was fond of rock and roll groups like the Beatles. So although the Beatles' songs became one of my song signs that I felt my dad was sending me, I was a bit surprised that additionally, when I'd pray to my dad, soon after, Pink Floyd would come on the radio. I then realized that the most often heard Pink Floyd song sign was "Wish You were Here." Well, there you have it -- it was not so much about connecting Pink Floyd with my dad, but our mutual message of love through wishing "he was here" by my side physically.

However, the financial stress was beginning to take its toll. First, I was trying to organize yet another Family Travel Marketing Expo, via my teen travel blog as a way to bring in some money. Expos necessitated long hours and were a financial gamble since I had to put money down for a venue yet there was no guarantee how many family travel vendors I'd get to participate and pay. Second, I was writing a monthly newsletter for a non-profit organization as yet another way to keep me afloat. However, often my information for writing the newsletter came in at the last minute and I'd have mere hours to turn it into a newsletter, all while being on campus, writing Shakespeare essays and parenting two children as a divorced parent. I knew that something had to give.

On September 10, I wrote in my journal, "I feel overwhelmed. I desire someone to help me figure this all out. I need a positive solution to my money situation that will come to me now." Soon after I went for a walk in the park and saw a blue heron which was a sign from my dad to be patient and have faith.

One of the first days on campus, I saw a poster for an upcoming jobs fair for students. I had visions of working in the cafeteria with a little white paper hat and knew that at my age, that just was not for me. However, right after seeing the jobs fair sign, I came across an outdoor sale of posters on campus. No surprise, there was a huge Eiffel Tower poster which of course I had to buy. It still adorns my bedroom door as a constant reminder to trust my personal symbols. Seeing this poster on campus affirmed for me that I should still go to next week's jobs fair and explore the options. Additionally, I wrote this affirmation down again while meditating that said, "I am taking a positive, abrupt turn down manifestation lane." When I got in my car soon after that, I turned on the radio and The Doors were playing. Music by The Doors is a positive song sign for me since I often would draw a picture of "doors" opening for me with ease -- as in opportunities coming my way.

Meanwhile, one of the requirements of getting any teaching certificate is passing the Praxis tests. While I ultimately wanted to teach high school English, I wanted to keep all my options open so that I would be more marketable. Thus, I did a crazy thing and signed up for six Praxis tests -- all given within a ten day period in early October! That way, once I passed them and got all my additional required credits, I would be qualified to teach high school, middle school and grammar school. My big concern was the grammar school Praxis since it contained four different subject areas including English, history, math and science; the latter two were not my forte. I hadn't had any math or science classes since junior year of high school. English, of course, was my strong point along with history, since I had learned so much about history and geography from my days as a travel writer. Inevitably I got a math tutor and felt it was worth paying for a few sessions in order to increase my chances of passing this portion of the test. Still, understanding higher level concepts like probability made me doubtful I'd pass the math and science parts of the Praxis tests on the first try.

I had very limited time to study for the Praxis since I was working two part time jobs, getting used to being in college again and parenting my two kids. Regarding science prep, I only had time to peruse this section; I figured I'd focus on the others and would probably fail science and have to take it again. The rule with Praxis tests is that all you need to do is pass each test in order to fulfill that part of teaching certification. Your individual scores do not get turned over to future employers.

However, I wrote in my journal how anxious I was getting about passing all six tests. Again, a few days later I again wrote the same guidance as before, "I am taking a positive, abrupt turn down manifestation lane. This message is being repeated for emphasis to help trust that it is all about to be seen! Trust the signs. Trust yourself.

67

I am going to do fine on the Praxis tests."

Next time I got into the car, the song "You Ain't Seen Nothin' Yet" was playing. This was quite an appropriate follow-up to what I had just written and soon this song was added to my growing list of song signs. And right after that, can you guess which song I heard? "Wish you were here" -- again.

LET IT BE

As each day went on, the stress was also building financially. On September 17, I wrote, "Please bring me part time or freelance writing or some type of decent paying work NOW so that I can leave my stressful freelance job AND obtain more financial security." Again, "Wish you were here" was heard on my radio that day. Two days later, the affirmation I wrote in my journal was, "I have not been forsaken! Keep trusting and moving forward. I'm doing so well, even if it might not feel that way right now. My financial concerns are being eased NOW! I don't have to know HOW it will happen. Instead, I just know that it is happening NOW." Although this helped at the time of writing it, I still felt so anxious anytime I had to pay a bill. The next day I wrote this affirmation in my journal before meditating, "The money is here and will give me the peace of mind that I need until I get a full time teaching job. Trust myself and my signs. I will not fall. The financial support is here and it's all going to work out in the long run with teaching." I came downstairs and what was playing on my kitchen radio? "Let it Be" -- my song signs of all song signs! The next day it was on my car radio when I started the car at which point I wrote in my journal, "Something big and positive is about to happen since I heard Let it Be two days in a row!"

My family has a long history of "Let it Be" as a sign. When my older brother was looking at St. Joseph's College in Philadelphia, the song "Let it Be" had just hit the airwaves. When we entered the chapel as we toured St. Joseph's, someone was practicing the organ there. When my mom heard that the organist was playing "Let it Be," she proclaimed to my brother, "It's a sign that you should come here to college!" Not only did my brother end up going to college there but my daughter Alex worked there in Campus Ministry about 40 years after my brother attended St. Joe's! That said, "Let it Be" has become one of my most enduring and dear signs of all since it has been a personal symbol for me since my childhood. In fact, just hearing it can bring me to tears!

Fast forward to life back at college for me as I raced to get my teaching certification. Finally, the day came for the jobs fair and amazingly, I secured an interview with a non-profit affiliated with the college. The part-time job had flexible hours, involved writing social media posts and rewriting copy for the group's healthy living/healthy eating website. It was right up my alley and thankfully I got the job! So the affirmations I kept writing in my journal and the song signs I kept hearing were right; I needed to trust and keep the faith that I was meant to get my teaching certificate. I am forever grateful to Laura of *Eat, Play, Live* for that opportunity which was such a big help in keeping me afloat. This gave me the courage to step down from my part time newsletter job and to also shelf another labor-intensive family travel marketing fair. I had my hands full as I ran my proverbially – and hopefully – eight-month marathon at Montclair State University. When I got home after securing the part time job, I accessed my Pandora music feed. What came on? "Let it Be"

Back to life at Montclair State University: September ended with me feeling a bit less anxious about finances and this big leap of faith I was taking. One of the affirmations I wrote in my journal after meditation at the end of the month said, "I'm experiencing MAJOR LIFE BREAKTHROUGHS this coming month...this season...this year! It may seem scary but the Universe is holding my hand and has got my back. It's all good." This was followed by a number of days in which I wrote in my journal that I was seeing HUGE signs, ranging from seeing lots of blue herons and snowy egrets in the park along with many 22's, and songs, songs, songs by The Beatles, Pink Floyd and more. A few days later I did indeed have a major breakthrough because after meditating, I wrote in my journal, "I think that one of the ways I'm going to get back on my feet financially, in addition to teaching, is writing a book about how the signs have guided me throughout so much change. Ah ha -- there is money IN ME and in these journal pages! Teaching will not only be a fulfilling career but will allow me to have summers to write my books on signs." It was hard to comprehend at that time that many years later, I'd really be doing just that!

YOUR TAKEAWAY

TIPS: When is a sign...a sign?

1. Practice makes better

It is not the intention of the Universe to tease us or bring us down a devastating path. The more you practice using signs for smaller decisions or affirmations at first, the more you will trust that Divine Orchestration is pointing you in the right direction to make bigger career and financial decisions.

2. Trust your gut

As the saying goes, there is no such thing as coincidence. Trust your gut -- that little voice inside you -- that the signs, helpful people and messages that are coming across your path are just what you need at the moment.

3. If something does not feel right deep down, then don't do it

Personal symbols were never meant to lead us into danger or dire consequences. True guidance from the Universe does not work that way. Never interpret signs as a means to rationalize hurting someone else or yourself intentionally.

4. Remember, to ask for a sign before you take a big step

Send to the Universe your intention of needing a sign of affirmation before you take a big step in your life. You will be amazed at how quickly a sign -- or signs -- will appear! The more you learn to read and trust signs, the less you will need to ask for them. After a few years of following my personal symbols, I rarely ask for them anymore -- they are present in every step I take!

CHAPTER 8
SONG SIGNS - PART 2
ROCKIN' THAT CASBAH!

The Final Stretch
Luisa Frey

You are beautiful, you are wise
You are in for an awesome surprise!

Woohoo, yeeha, yay, and all that
Soon you'll be feeling like you are top cat –

A beautiful cat who made it to the top
It's been a "marathon" and you never once did stop

Instead you kept going, energized by your mission
And now positive manifestation *has come* to fruition.

Yes, "has come" we did say, because the deal is done –
You're about to get a teaching job next September – you've won!

You'll blossom and thrive to say the least
And have the financial means for a celebratory feast!

You can manage teaching a class and keeping the pace
Gone are your worries – without a trace.

And the time to shine is now, now, now!
You're ready and so is your employer and students – oh wow!

You'll be "Rockin' the Casbah" all the way to the bank
And you have only yourself to really thank

Because YOU kept the faith even when things looked grim
YOU persevered through thick and thin

YOU trusted your signs and your very own voice
And ultimately made the right, new career choice.

In the meantime, stay the course for the finish line is in sight

We'll keep you energized and your final exams will be "A's" – dyn-o-mite!

Go now, the final stretch is finally here

Visualize that finish line and let out a BIG CHEER!

Rockin' That Casbah!

Soon enough, early October came when I had to take the six Praxis tests over a period of ten days. Things had changed since I had taken SAT's 35 years earlier, for now standardized tests were online with a timer constantly ticking in your face. It was also a bit unnerving to have to undergo stringent security before entering the testing site. I could not even bring a water bottle into the testing room. When I came back from the first of my six tests, I wrote in my journal, "The science test was soooo much harder than those in the practice books. There was so much physics on it which I never had in school. Please let me pass!"

The next morning I went to Starbucks wearing my "Let it Be" shirt as a type of good luck charm. Wouldn't you know it but the guy in line behind me had a "Pink Floyd" shirt on! So. although I was not hearing the songs, they were still ever-present signs telling me to keep the faith!

I took the history Praxis which was not so bad, nor were the three English tests. (Note: I had to take THREE different English Praxis tests -- one for each level of school I wanted to be certified in: grammar, middle and high school.) Last up was my nemesis: math. I had forgotten test taking strategies over the years and spent too much time on problems I did not know. I didn't even get to finish the last few problems before time ran out. I felt great despair as I left the testing site. However, I had my car packed to go right from the testing site to visit my daughter Alex at her college. As I got into the car and turned on the ignition, my magic radio was playing "Girls Just Wanna' have Fun" by Cindy Lauper. It was the release I needed after the intensive ten days of testing. Soon enough I was fist pumping to the song as I drove off to Boston!

During the wait for my Praxis test scores to be published online, I kept hearing "Rock the Casbah" by the Clash over and over again every time I'd turn on the radio. I am a rock and roller at heart so the word "rock" in the title has many positive connotations for me. One of the times I heard it was right after paying bills, which I especially hated during this time period due to how tight my finances were. Hearing the song lifted my spirits for sure. The song "Rock the Casbah" is about a Middle Eastern sheik ordering his people not to listen to Western rock and roll music. However, the people followed their hearts (and tapping toes) and were defiant of the sheik; they kept rockin' that casbah until the sheik gave up. When applying this song metaphorically to my situation, there were plenty of good reasons why my endeavors to change my career might not work out in the end but I, like the people in this song, was defiant of those demands and remained true to my heart and desires.

Once back home, while waiting for my Praxis scores, I kept hearing another song on my radio, "Don't Stop Believing" and in fact I heard it on November 1 and 3. Then on November 4, I was finally able to access my Praxis test scores online. I assumed that I passed the history and three English tests but not the science and math. Upon looking at the scores I started crying. But wait -- it's not what you think. I was crying tears of joy because I PASSED ALL SIX PRAXIS TESTS -- EVEN MATH AND SCIENCE!

In my tears, I thanked my dad up in heaven for his help since he was always very good in math and he kept sending me signs during this process. The remarkable part is that I passed math by only one point…only one point! But all I needed to do was pass, and that I did. Once again, I see how the signs that directed me and supported me on this challenging path to "Don't Stop Believing" had not failed me.

I was thoroughly enjoying my English classes during the fall semester and also signed up for an interim online course between semesters to make sure I would obtain the 30 needed credits to teach high school English, which was my first choice in teaching. You see, I was still in limbo as to how many English credits the NJDOE would approve from my Boston College transcript.

Despite many, many emails, letters and calls to NJDOE, my transcript – that I sent early September – still had not been reviewed. I was operating in the dark without the knowledge of whether I'd be able to fulfill all the credits needed to finish up by May. It was a miracle I was able to pay my bills so far but I could not imagine keeping this financial tightrope up for more than a year. Obviously with teaching, you need to be in the market by spring (have your teaching certificate on its way) in order to procure interviews for the upcoming September school year.

As I entered the winter semester, a little voice inside me said to take three English classes this semester instead of two in order to hedge my bets that I'd have enough credits once NJDOE *finally* got around to reviewing my college transcript. However, taking more than three would not have been possible financially or timewise, due to my part time job and family responsibilities.

WHEN IN DOUBT, LOOK FOR THE SIGNS

As the winter months wore on and still there was no confirmation from NJDOE regarding which Boston College classes would go towards my certification, I began to doubt my signs. What if I read them wrong? What if I needed more than the 18 credits I took that year? What if NJDOE did not approve my journalism classes to be counted towards English credits? But the signs and affirmative messages kept coming louder and clearer.

For example, at one point when I was doubting whether I could pull this whole thing off, I wrote down this affirmative message after meditating, "I have not been forsaken even though it sometimes feels that way. I am about to see a CAVALCADE of beautiful things come to me and they will be here to stay. I need to stay the course." After I wrote this, I went out to do an errand and a woman walked by me holding a dozen roses, which as noted before, is a big personal symbol. Soon after that I wrote in my journal that I feel that my life is "about to take an abrupt turn down positive manifestation street" despite it not looking like that on the surface at the moment. The next morning as I got on the highway to go to classes, a truck passed me that said in big letters, "VICTORY 22" As you recall, 22 is one of my major signs so this helped me get back to a place of hopefulness.

A few weeks later, I still had not heard back from NJDOE and was again not trusting that my plan of getting my certification in a year would really occur. I wrote the affirmation in my journal that I am about to experience "enormous positive changes." Naturally, I got signs of affirmation immediately when I heard the band "Chicago" on the radio as well as saw Paul McCartney and Ringo Starr perform at the Grammys. You can't get a more in-your-face Beatles sign than that!

As March progressed, I was in the home stretch of my school year at MSU, yet NJDOE still had not reviewed my transcript.

At that point, I called them with fire in my belly and demanded that it be reviewed immediately, since I had paid my fees for that service the prior fall. The next day, I wrote this affirmation in my journal, "Something big and beautiful is about to be seen in my life!" Naturally, everywhere I looked the rest of the day, I saw the 22 constantly. Once again, my signs and affirmations, along with my action of calling NJDOE, got me back to a place of positivity.

As I was still extremely stressed about my finances, I got approved to refinance my mortgage. I was not sure this would really go through due to my part-time employment; however, it did. This refinance not only gave me some cash in my pocket but also allowed me to pay for college tuition yet again for my daughter. I was worrying about my schoolwork, attracting a teaching job, and my finances so I sat down to meditate to get in a better place emotionally. I then wrote in my journal, "I know deep in my gut that teaching is meant to be. It is NOT a gamble! See how things keep falling into place...Let it Be!" This of course was affirmed by hearing "Wish you were here" along with a plethora of Beatles songs the rest of the day.

By this time it was late March and I needed to start sending out resumes for teaching jobs -- yet I still was unsure if I had enough credits to get my high school English certification, due to lack of communication with NJDOE. However, I had just seen "mega signs" in a matter of an hour including the following signs: 22 (many times), Beatles songs, cardinal and roses. And yes, "Rockin' the Casbah" just so happened to be once again blaring on my radio when I got into my car. The next day, after meditating, I wrote in my journal, "There are many beautiful things about to emerge inside of me and also in the outside world. They are manifesting now which is about to change my life positively forever!" I truly FELT this affirmation deep down despite being in limbo still since the signs helped me feel it all was about to manifest.

Wouldn't you know it, but later that day I finally got a call from NJDOE. I remember where I was when I received the call because so much of my future was in the hands of NJDOE's decision. The bad news: my many journalism classes would not count as English classes. It was hard to fathom that, as a future high school English teacher, all that I learned from journalism classes, as well as my already 30 years as a professional journalist, would not count towards teaching English. However, the very good news was that NJDOE approved 12 English credits from Boston College. And those 12 credits plus the 18 credits I was finishing up at MSU equaled the 30 credits needed for certification to teach high school English! The impossible was possible! And once again, I shed tears of joy and thankfulness at this amazing news.

I had now jumped through every difficult hurdle in a mere eight months. I was really going to get certified to teach high school English, middle school English and grammar school. Now the "only" big hurdle left was to get a teaching job for September.

YOUR TAKEAWAY

Your Thoughts Count!

YOU are the most important part of the process of learning how to interpret signs. Below are some questions for you to answer; by doing so it will help you learn how to process the signs you are seeing and hearing.

We all have the ability to tap into our gut, which is known as our intuition. The more we do, the easier it is for us to interpret the signs which appear in our lives. These questions will help get you started on being more aware and confident in listening to and following your intuition. It is important to be in tune with how you receive "knowingness" since you can tap into this to help you interpret signs you receive.

1. Describe something you "knew" was going to happen before it happened. It can be as simple as thinking of a person and then they contact you later that day or week.

_____

_____

_____

2.Where were you when you had a feeling that something was going to happen and then later it did: (Was it in a dream? While outdoors? During meditation? Etc.)

_____

_____

_____

3. How did you "know" it was going to happen? Did you: (check one)

3a. Feel it in your gut? _____

3b. Hear a little voice inside telling you to do or not do something?

_____

Now use this knowledge to help you be more aware to "trust your gut" next time you get an intuitive "hit."

CHAPTER 9

ROSES REPRISE: BACK TO WHERE IT ALL BEGAN

I think I can, I think I can, I knew I could, I knew I could

(Title from The Little Engine that Could)

Luisa Frey

This poem, dear friend, is meant for you

Remember, you're not alone no matter what you do.

You've got lots now to think about and ponder

Weighty things that have not left you even when you travel and wander.

But your wandering days are ready to take a bow and say adieu
Because you are capable of doing what you know you have to do.

You are strong, much stronger than ever before
And it's this strength that will easily help you open up the door

For doors are never meant to be kept shut forever
Instead, they are meant to be walked through whenever…

…whenever YOU feel you can no longer survive, nor thrive, this way
Rest assured, that's when you'll be supported by friends each and
every day.

For we all only get one chance in this lifetime to go around
But this, you know, and are now ready for your heart to be found…

…found, released from the past and opened up wide
Look, see the jewels shining inside!

You may not think it, but you have diamonds just waiting to be seen
And appreciated and cherished by people who are always on your
"team".

You were meant to be happy, now and forever

By an employer --- and a paycheck -- that are present in fair or rocky weather.

But even after a big, dark storm, look how the sunshine streams in

To help you focus on the light and not where you've been.

As another year draws to a close we all tend to look back

When actually, we should focus on the beauty that's ahead in our track

And on this track, a train whistle is blowing and creating lots of steam

Get ready, hop aboard, embrace the journey to manifest your dreams!

ORIGAMI ROSES

The task of finding a teaching job was very tech-heavy and was a new endeavor for me since, in the past, the freelance jobs I got were usually through networking. I did have concerns that perhaps school districts would not be interested in me since I had not gone the traditional route of four years of undergraduate educational instruction nor had I done half a year of student teaching. Instead, though, I did have close to 30 years of professional writing experience and was positioning myself as a writing instructor.

On April 15, I wrote in my journal this affirmation after meditating: "BIG beautiful things are falling into my lap now. My light is so strong and is only attracting positive things. I am ready." The next day I recorded the following signs in rapid succession: "Don't Stop Believing" was heard on the radio, #22 was seen, I received a card with a blue butterfly on it, then I heard many Beatles songs, Pink Floyd's "Wish you were Here, " more Beatles songs, more #22's, and lastly saw roses on someone's T-shirt. As the signs were trying to communicate to me, things were about to shift since later that day, I got a call for a teaching job interview for English at a new charter middle school in a nearby inner city. Right after the call, I got into my car and heard "Let it Be." Now that is how signs sometimes work: first, an affirmation that I write or feel or sense; many signs to confirm that affirmation; and then the positive action occurring all in rapid succession. On the day of the interview, I saw the following signs: #22, Eiffel Tower/Paris, a single pink rose randomly found on the sidewalk, a cardinal, Pink Floyd and the only parking spot left at the school when I pulled up for the interview was 2222! The interview went well and I had a feeling I'd hear from them again for future interviews.

The last day of classes arrived at Montclair State University and I was actively seeking teaching jobs, knowing that this summer my provisional teaching certificate would arrive. The day after classes ended, I got many signs that I felt were about future teaching interviews and ultimately a job. These include Beatles songs and two Pink Floyd songs. Then when I was at Starbucks studying for my final exams, I asked one of the baristas who loved the Beatles to give me an inspirational quote. I thought it'd be a line from a Beatles song however, it was instead from a 13th-century poet and theologian named Rumi. The quote was so appropriate: "That which you seek is actually seeking you!" And voila – the following day I got a call for the third interview at the charter school; this time I'd have to do an English lesson whereby I'd be teaching a demo class to sixth graders. So in effect, that which I was seeking was indeed seeking and pursuing me. I was happy that the teaching demo went quite well, the students found me engaging and that I felt very comfortable being in front of a class of 25 students.

The following week while I was meditating, I saw a visual of me, my house, and my checkbook all covered with roses! Surely that was a good sign -- and of course it was since a few hours later I got an email from the charter school CFO that she wanted to talk to me about employment! WOOHOO! Finally, I had reached the finish line of my nine-month marathon and felt like I was wearing that crown of leaves like the triumphant ancient Greek marathoners did!

The summer was one filled with plans to get ready for the pace of my new career, but surely there was a feeling of relief too for all that I had accomplished in the past nine months. However, I was at the end of my financial resources. I had my part-time job through the summer, but my credit cards were accruing and my resources were totally tapped out. I know that the Universe truly had my back since, when I got my first paycheck that September from teaching, I had a mere $597 in my bank account. My journey of following the signs to a new career had manifested into reality just in the nick of time!

We teachers had to start back to school two weeks early for training and workshops. I was very disconcerted when we had a full day of training on how to physically defend oneself against aggressive students as well as multiple workshops focused on discipline. However, when I walked around the city neighborhood, I was "heartened" by the red "hearts" painted in random places on the sidewalk and nearby buildings. I took this as a good sign that as long as my heart is aligned with the mission of teaching, that it will all work out -- no matter what it's like when my students walk into my classroom. Finally the big day arrived, and as I drove to school I heard on the radio "Don't stop believing," Beatles songs and had seen multiple 22's -- all good signs.

However, like the majority of my fellow teachers, I found the behavior of my 27 students per class to be extremely difficult to handle. There was little respect and not much desire to learn. The students at our school faced multiple, tough challenges in their difficult home life which was all brought into the classroom daily. I was so dismayed and stressed since I kept trying different ways to manage my classes but still there was little time for teaching since most of my time dealt with behavioral issues.

One week into the job, I put out feelers to some of my educational contacts to see if there were any maternity leave jobs elsewhere since I did not feel I would last a whole year in this stressful teaching environment. I was beyond disappointed since I had put so much effort into getting to this point. However, after meditation I wrote this affirmation down: "I have NOT been brought this far for me to fall now. The Universe will either help me deal with my students' behavior or will bring me a new opportunity." The next day I wrote this subsequent affirmation in my journal: "The Universe and I are co-creating a new teaching environment very quickly -- certainly within the coming year -- in which I'll thrive and not just survive. It is going to get better."

The next day the principal came to my classroom and asked me to come see him; he had a fellow teacher cover my classroom. I was nervous since I did not know why he wanted to speak with me, however, it turned out to be a blessing in disguise. Due to major scheduling problems, the school had to pull out one English and one math teacher from teaching the big classes and make them remedial, small group instructors as well as push-in instructors. (Push-in is when teachers quietly aid remedial students while the lead teacher is teaching in order to keep the struggling students on task and support their needs.) And yup, the English teacher being pulled out of the big class mayhem was me! I was so thankful since I felt that remedial work and small group instruction would lend itself to more real teaching and less focus on behavior.

When I returned to my classroom and desk after this short meeting, there was a HUGE personal symbol for me on my desk, affirming that remedial English was where I was supposed to be: one of my students had made me an origami vase (out of paper) filled with THREE ROSES!!! It took my breath away since it was an instant affirmation that even though I never thought of focusing my teaching efforts solely on students with reading and writing challenges, this change was where I was going to shine. Receiving that instant rose sign once again elicited the following response from my friend Dr. John, "You can't make this stuff up!"

I started remedial, small group instruction right away and after the first day I wrote in my journal that "I am now on easy street. My career and vocation are in alignment with my heart. I'm going to shine, shine, shine! I'm going to help so many kids and I will thrive on that energy. I'm where I'm supposed to be." Indeed I felt like I was finally truly teaching and there was minimal need to focus on behavior. I really looked forward to my small group time in the afternoon. Additionally, I was learning a lot from observing one of the seasoned English teachers whose classroom I pushed into in the morning.

IF AT FIRST YOU DON'T SUCCEED, TRY, TRY AGAIN!

However, the school refused to spend the money on substitute teachers and so I was constantly being asked at the last minute to cancel my small group instruction or give up lunch periods to substitute in all subjects. The students' behavior for subs was extremely disrespectful and I felt like I had to be someone I was not when I was subbing for other people. This was totally not my style.

When I meditated at home, I kept hearing this affirmation: "Something big and beautiful is about to happen to you that will make your days easier." This occurred three days in a row and then was followed by the abrupt news that the school was running out of funds and was laying off non-essential staff. This included me since now that I was in small group support it was considered non-essential – this included my fellow math remedial/push-in teacher and a number of other support staff. When I was told this, rather than freaking out at the fact that I so needed a regular paycheck, my shoulders relaxed and I let out a sigh of relief. I recalled the messages I had been writing after meditation about something big and beautiful about to happen and that helped me realize that this school is NOT where I am supposed to be in order to make a difference and to feel appreciated. I wrote in my journal that night that "I know that God is closing this window and opening a bigger and more beautiful door for me. " I got immediate signs that this was meant to be including #22, Eiffel Tower, hearing "Let it Be" and "Wish You Were Here" and many significant other Beatles songs.

The days following were filled with moments of panic (OMG -- where am I going to find a full-time teaching job just a few months into the school year?) as well as many meditation-inspired affirmations written in my journal that were the opposite of panic. They were quite profuse; one, for example, was "Right now, something positive is configuring regarding employment which will fit me like a glove!" The signs kept coming too which helped me keep the faith. I had a few interviews but they were either for short-term teaching jobs without benefits or hourly remedial teaching. How was I going to pay my bills once again let alone keep my daughter in an expensive private college? I had been given two months' notice at the city school and would be employed until right before Christmas. The race to find a new teaching job was on.

Meanwhile it was chaotic at the city school. We kept getting mixed messages that the school was going to find some money so that those of us who got the pink slip would be able to stay on for the year. While the remedial positions did get reinstated, the school board gave our principal a cryptic message that they still had not approved who would teach those newly re-approved remedial courses. Huh? Our attempts at clarification were ignored and we felt extremely disregarded and disrespected. Once again, the signs and meditation-inspired affirmations I wrote in my journals were telling me that I deserved to be treated better and that limbo was NOT where I wanted to be. And so I kept pounding the pavement for a new teaching position elsewhere since the clock was indeed ticking away.

During this time of uncertainty, I was in a store one day and saw the following logos/signs on sweaters on a shelf: *Rose, heart, Eiffel Tower, rose, Eiffel Tower.*

I felt that the Universe was giving me a message through those sweater signs and I interpreted it like this: "Follow your intuition and heart to your Eiffel Tower -- that which they said you could not do, but where you know you're supposed to be." The following day I got a call from a Modern Jewish Orthodox high school to come in for an interview for a full-time job to replace someone who was retiring.

This school is a Yeshiva, which means that it is both an academic high school plus includes about four periods a day of Judaic studies. It is located in a New Jersey county where I had always felt that I'd end up teaching at a private high school. In fact, I had sent out a lot of resumes to private Catholic high schools in that county during my initial job search since I was following my intuition which told me I'd feel comfortable teaching in a private high school in that county. Well, the Catholic schools had no available positions but sure enough, a Modern Jewish Orthodox high school in the county I was drawn to did have a job opening.

The interview with the Yeshiva school was on November 21 and it went quite well. In fact, the person interviewing me went to the same high school as me, I just so happened to know her niece, and her great nephew used to play with my son when they were toddlers! The position entailed teaching four periods of remedial, small group instruction which would support other English and history teachers, as well as teaching two periods a day of my own big English classes for 9th and 11th graders with learning challenges. Now mind you, I was not Special Ed certified, however, due to my experience at the city school with small group, remedial/special needs students, I was being considered for the job. I loved the atmosphere and energy of the Yeshiva school; there were beautiful religious murals and stained-glass windows bringing in lots of light. The interview went quite well and the next day when I meditated, I saw roses all around me.

However, the days ticked by and I surprisingly did not hear back from the Yeshiva school despite very positive feedback during and after the interview. Since it was not a sure thing and soon I'd be unemployed, I also went on an interview at a public school for small group instruction that would only be paid on a part time and hourly basis. Conversely, the Yeshiva would be full time with benefits. During this time I wrote in my journal this meditation-inspired affirmation: "Do not fret, do not fear, do not resist. I'll see quite soon what is meant to be. I'll end up teaching somewhere where I am meant to be." I then wrote that I saw myself teaching under a grove of trees. This message was then followed by hearing "Let it Be" on the radio, of course.

In the meantime, the charter school kept giving us cryptic, mixed messages about possible continued employment there. It was not only frustrating but did not feel like I was a priority there at all. On November 30, despite not hearing a word back from the Yeshiva, my first choice by far, I wrote the following meditation-inspired affirmation in my journal: "There is a BIG opening I'm going to slip into with ease -- it's a great fit for me and will give me fulfillment, the money that I need, and job security." I got into the car and "Let it Be" was on -- again! These affirmations and constant hearing of "Let it Be" helped me keep the faith for sure.

On December 8, despite no reply from my email to my interviewer at the Yeshiva, when I meditated, I saw myself surrounded by roses. Since the Yeshiva was not replying to my email, I had made an appointment for the following day to accept and sign the contract for the part-time, hourly remedial work at the public school. This was NOT financially ideal to say the least and it was not the positive environment that I felt while at the Yeshiva.

YOUR TAKEAWAY

Your Thoughts Count!

YOU are the most important part of the process of learning how to interpret signs. Below are more quick questions for you to consider and answer, by doing so it will help you learn how to process the signs you are seeing and hearing.

The questions below focus on your feelings towards where you work and what you do professionally.

1. How do you FEEL when you walk into the place where you work? Is it positive energy, negative or no energy at all?

_____

_____

2. If you work out of a home office, how do you FEEL when you either walk into the area where you work on your computer or when you start your computer that day? (Example, when I walked into my home office nine months before I went back to school for teaching

certification, in my heart I knew that I did not want to be working alone anymore in this freelance capacity).

_____

_____

3. What aspects of your job do you like or enjoy? It can be the people, the tasks or the money/benefits.

_____

_____

4. What aspects of your job do you NOT like or enjoy? It can be the people, the tasks or the money/benefits.

_____

_____

5. Do the aspects that you like outweigh those that you do NOT like?

_____ Yes   OR _____ No

6. If the positive aspects do NOT outweigh the negative, might you consider the following (check those that apply).

_____Journaling about signs that you are receiving

_____ Talking to a career coach about looking for new employment that is more in alignment with who you truly are

_____ Starting to actively explore other employment options by looking at what is available online for either your present field OR an area you have always wanted to possibly work in

_____Going back to school to get whatever degree or training necessary to make an employment move

7. For any areas you checked off above, write down which two first steps you feel most comfortable exploring.

7a.

_____

_____

7b.

_____

_____

8. Might you really take the steps noted above? Please be honest with yourself.

_____Yes OR _____No

If the answer is yes, consider getting a journal to help you record your thoughts, actions and the signs that you see and hear along the way!

If the answer is no, try to find some quiet time so that you can explore why you don't want to take any steps towards exploring other career options despite possible lack of positivity in the workplace.

CHAPTER 10
EVERYTHING'S COMING UP ROSES
Luisa Frey

Your glory days are peeking out over the horizon for sure

Just a few more steps 'til we break down any last closed doors

The winds of change have blown through your life with gale force

And now it's time to sit back and allow them to take their course...

...With the final goal: your positive manifestation

Of all your dreams -- truly cause for celebration!

The table is being set for the big feast that's about to come

Even though you can't see it, your trophy has already been won!

Go now in continued faith that it's all unfolding according to plan

And feel energized by the hurdles you jumped and the miles you ran.

ROSES POISED TO BLOOM

The night before I was about to sign the other contract, I got an email from my interviewer at the Yeshiva who said she had not been in touch due to unexpected travel. She then wrote, "I'm very interested in hiring you. I checked with my niece and she says you are terrific!" My last step was to meet the principal and hopefully seal the deal. Two days later, and a mere three days before the last day at the city school, I got the job at the Yeshiva school! I was so thrilled and thankful! There were so many signs that day that affirmed that this is where I was supposed to be: #22, many songs by The Doors, Pink Floyd, "Don't stop believing", and even a photo of a cardinal on a candy wrapper randomly seen while on my park walk.

My last day at the city school was filled with a lot of emotions since part of me was relieved yet the other part of me felt like I was letting these kids down. Their lives were so full of adults walking out on them and I felt badly that I was yet another adult doing that. Thus, I wrote them a farewell poem; I was a bit emotional reading it to each of my classes. The students presented me beautiful handmade goodbye cards that brought me to tears. That night, the meditation-inspired message I wrote in my journal made me feel better: "I cared about those kids and that's all that mattered!"

Over the Christmas holidays, I had time to relax and prepare for round two of my first action-packed year of teaching. As I was unpacking Christmas ornaments, I found a little holiday card I wrote to myself a year earlier on 12/24/13 -- it was an affirmation at that time of what I desired to have in my life by 12/24/14. Here's what it said:

"Easy street is here -- hooray! I have a job aligned with my heart's desire...I have financial security...life is good...amen!"

And indeed, what I had written a year earlier had just come to fruition with my acceptance of the remedial English teaching position at the Yeshiva.

WHERE I AM SUPPOSED TO BE

I started the new year of 2015 off on a great note and wrote in my journal on 1/3/15: "Good first day of school! I have a lot to learn but I truly feel that this school and this position is a good fit. Yay!" The next day I wrote all the wonderful signs of affirmation I received after my first day of school at the Yeshiva including: F22 on a license plate on a car parked by mine in school, Pink Floyd and lots of Beatles songs. To top it off, a replica Eiffel Tower was given to me by one of my son's friends as a thank you for driving him around while his mom was out of the country. The Eiffel Tower even lit up! This, I felt, was symbolic about how teaching at the Yeshiva was lighting up my life.

Right away, I saw a desire and motivation in my students to learn despite how difficult reading comprehension and writing essays was for them. I thrive on working with someone who is motivated, no matter how much they may struggle to master the material at hand. I was finding that all my years of having my own writing/marketing/social media business definitely aided me in teaching challenged students since I was used to figuring out how to break down new tasks in my business in order to accomplish them. I used this principle extensively with my students and it was working like a charm.

Of course, as is natural, I did feel some anxiety of getting used to my schedule since, at the Yeshiva, I never taught in the same room two periods in a row. Additionally, I had to quickly get up to speed to support students in small groups who were reading novels I had not read yet -- nor did I have much time to read them at that moment. However, during the first week there I wrote in my journal this meditation-inspired message, "DO NOT fret! I am meant to be here for many reasons that I will soon see. They'll love me here and I am going to shine here!" The next day, while I was in my office room at school, I overheard some students in the hallway playing the guitar...could that really be..."Let it Be?" Indeed it was! That affirmation of all affirmations was exactly what I needed to help me feel more confident and less anxious as I started this new adventure.

As I sit to write this chapter, I have noticed an uncanny thing I wrote and drew in my journal from when I was going to Montclair State University in the winter of 2014 and was very much in the fear stage regarding finances. One of the affirmations I wrote in my journal at that time was that "I am very well protected. I am letting go of money fears, concerns about my college classes and stress about getting a teaching job. **It is all mapped out as well as plan A,B,C,D,E.** I will not fall. I have found my calling and now it is being brought home to me!"

What is so synchronistic about this message is that over a year later when I started teaching at the Yeshiva, I prayed to be enlightened regarding ways to best teach learning-challenged students how to write college-level essays. The day after my prayer, I came up with a thunderbolt of an idea which I named the ABCDE pattern of writing. It has since worked wonders with improving hundreds of my students' writing; students and teachers alike in my school know it as ABCDE format of writing. I had no recall of ever writing the affirmation in 2014 about "plan A,B,C,D,E" when I created the ABCDE methodology of writing over a year later in 2015. I do indeed feel that it was sent from above since it has turned students' writing around remarkably and has helped students become confident and competent essay writers.

Additionally, I have noticed two other interesting synchronicities from the past, while presently writing this book. When I was in great flux over the impending end of my job at the city school, I wrote in my journal that I saw myself in a grove of trees. Well, I just realized that indeed the first spring I taught at the Yeshiva, I took my juniors out to discuss *The Great Gatsby* on benches that are under a grove of trees! Additionally, in late January of 2015 -- a few weeks after starting my job at the Yeshiva, I wrote the following message of affirmation in my journal: "I am like a strong, beautiful tree when it comes to teaching since, like a tree, I have strong limbs, I am flexible, students and parents will want to sit under my proverbial 'shade' and I am growing and beautiful inside." Again the image of a grove of trees was on my mind since I drew trees in my journal. And at that time, I had never seen the Yeshiva in bloom to realize that there indeed was a grove of trees!

What's most important, though, is the realization that although it was so incredibly hard to keep the faith with all the stress and drama of my first teaching job in the city school, following my signs led me to where I was exactly supposed to be. Had I not had the experience of remedial instruction at the city school, I would not have been qualified to get the job at the Yeshiva. Had I not had the experience of having my own travel writing/marketing/social media business, with all its challenges and financial stresses, I would not have been so resourceful and quick on my feet when I started teaching at the Yeshiva mid-year. While on the surface one might think that the signs lead me astray in regards to pointing me first to the city school, they did not. The signs indeed led me to where I was supposed to be, which is teaching English to high school students with learning challenges.

SHOWER OF ROSES

And so the shower of proverbial roses from St. Therese began quite soon after I started teaching at the Yeshiva. For example, while I was correcting my first set of papers, I had Pandora music on my computer and of course, "Let it Be" randomly came on. A few weeks later, the proverbial shower of roses continued during a big staff meeting. The principal paused at the beginning of the meeting to introduce me and told the staff how much the kids and parents like me already. I was so incredibly relieved to hear that especially due to my first, challenging experience in the city school. I then looked down at the wrapper of the tea bag that I grabbed on the coffee table that had been set up for teachers and the wrapper said that the tea was "ROSE chai." (Two things that I love -- roses and chai tea!)

The school year continued and while it was a huge learning curve with tons of time spent at night and on weekends with lesson planning and correcting essays, my confidence continued to grow, as did my students'. Finally, the day arrived for my first "Gallery Walk" which has since become a trademark project I assign annually in all my big English classes. Here is how a Gallery Walk works: I choose a broad time period that relates to the book we are reading (Example: 1960's which ties into "Secret Life of Bees" novel which is set in Civil Rights South). I then assign each student a topic related to the broad subject (Example: music of the 1960's, Civil Rights leaders, Jim Crow laws, etc.). I try to tailor each topic to each student's interests and abilities too. Students then have to research their topics, write a few paragraphs on that research and put that info on a poster board or other medium featuring creative visuals.

The day of the Gallery Walk is when students bring their projects in, and we display them in the classroom, as students walk around critiquing each project. Since my students struggle with organization and focus, I was concerned about not only their end product but also how they'd behave during the Gallery Walk. My fears were allayed since it was a big success! Needless to say, one of the students' projects had a few of my personal symbols on it; her topic was music of the 1960's and she included images of the Beatles, the Doors, and more.

The positive atmosphere continued. On April 18, I wrote in my journal that I have been receiving mega signs ranging from a cardinal flying right up to me outside my house to getting mailings from the St. Therese Society and even seeing a rose image randomly pop up on my computer. A great thing then transpired: my teaching contract for the following year was then renewed -- phew! More relief quickly followed in that I finished my Alternate Route night classes. (In order to "graduate" from the Provisional Teaching Certificate received from NJDOE after my coursework, to a Standard Teaching Certificate, we Alternate Route candidates had to take a year's worth of nighttime classes.)

This was a heavy load that was on top of lesson planning and correcting papers that are all part of a new Alternate Route teacher's duties. Therefore, another one of the big weights of this past year was lifted off my shoulders by completion of the Alternate Route night classwork.

That same day my supervisor told me that the father of one of my students said how much I'd helped his son learn to write in the past four months that I had him in class. Again, I felt like I was being showered with proverbial roses, and soon I literally was showered with roses, since my two children sent me roses for Mother's Day – this is something they did not normally do. The note said, "Since we know how you love roses, we thought we'd send you some from your 'two favorite roses.' We love you and ARE VERY PROUD OF YOU!" Wow, my kids were proud of me and all my efforts of the past year. I felt so incredibly blessed!

Right after that, I wrote the following meditation-inspired message in my journal that helped me rectify some confusion I was having --

and you, the reader, might one day have when you are following your signs -- about when signs point you in a direction but the immediate result is not necessarily a positive-feeling one. My message said,

"All the signs I got over the past six years for things that I felt, at first glance, did not work out -- be it related to career or relationships -- were still signs. They have led me to where I am supposed to be, as in teaching remedial English. If I did not have my own business and did not take the job at the city school, I would not be so competent and well equipped for what I am doing now."

That finally made a lot of sense out of signs I had recorded over the years where the positive outcome was not necessarily seen immediately.

Right after that, I literally saw a shower of roses. I went to the end of the year students' art show at my school. As I was running back to class, I spotted an amazing, huge painting by a student. The painting was a little village covered with snow but the main focus was of a literal shower of roses falling from the sky. I gulped -- you couldn't get a more obvious sign! It was affirming that the stressful journey of the past two years to get to this point was well worth it. I found out who painted it and asked her if I could pay her to make a copy of the painting and she obliged.

The next week was my annual end of the year meeting with our principal. It was so incredibly affirming since he said that my students and their parents were so happy to have me as their teacher, and that I have a kind way about me that is a perfect fit for my students' special needs. Lastly he said that I am part of the school's "family" and that they looked forward to having me stay on for future years to come! That same day, the student who drew the painting of the shower of roses walked into my room to affirm that her parents said that she can make a copy of the painting for me. You can't get a more blatant sign of affirmation than that! Later that night, I wrote in my journal, "HIP, HIP HOORAY! I finally feel like I am *home*."

June was a whirlwind of tying up things for the school year as well as creating/writing and correcting final exams for the first time. In the midst of this hectic atmosphere, I got such a beautiful email from the mother of one of my 11th grade students (named K here for privacy's sake). Her daughter had a tough time in English before I came to the Yeshiva. However, the ABCDE format of writing as well as my lessons in extensive annotating gave her visible confidence in her writing and comprehension abilities. The mom actually sent the email to my principal and cc'd me:

Dear Ms. Frey:

Thank you for finding my butterfly, for seeing her beauty and helping her spread her wings. We are eternally grateful for the spark you put in K's eyes and for keeping it shining and bright over the past year. Even when she would be overwhelmed and her shine would start to fade, you were always the one to get it to sparkle over again. Thank you for being K's teacher, her mentor, her comfort and her compass.

After I read this, I cried tears of joy! I then wrote in my journal, "This beautiful note affirmed, once again, that I made the right choices the past two years. Even though it has not been an easy path, this niche is where I'm supposed to be!" I then got immediate signs of affirmation: "Wish you were here" came on the radio, followed by "Here Comes the Sun" and then a butterfly flew right into my face.

Finally, the last day of school arrived -- I made it to the finish line with flying colors! If you had asked me if that would be possible last fall when the walls of my teaching dreams seemed to be crumbling down in the city school, I would have said "NO!" However the signs always gave me the faith to keep going.

What a beautiful last day of the school year. First, a freshman student came up to me to say how my confidence in him helped him gain confidence to work hard on the ABCDE pattern of writing. (Three years later he brought tears to my eyes when he told me on graduation night that if it were not for me teaching him how to write an essay, he would not have been able to go to college. He knew that one has to know how to write an essay in order to succeed in college.) And as I was shutting the light in my school office to head to our year-end teacher appreciation lunch, the student who painted the shower of roses brought in a copy of the painting for me -- it was gorgeous! It still adorns my home to this day.

But the biggest surprise was when the principal read, to the entire staff during our staff appreciation lunch, the email that the above-mentioned parent sent to him about how I helped her daughter succeed. I was glad he did not mention my name since I was a newbie there, but I quietly shed tears of joy and thanksgiving upon hearing this letter read by my principal. I was home. I was safe. I was being paid well. I was appreciated. I was making a difference. I was happy. I was -- and am -- a living testament that following the signs can lead to an amazingly beautiful life!

And so, "Let it Be…"

ABOUT THE AUTHOR

Luisa Frey, a high school English teacher, writing tutor and former professional travel writer, has been aware of signs (aka: personal symbols) since she was a little girl.

It was 1970 and the Beatles' *Let it Be* had just hit the charts. Her family was touring a college campus that her older brother was considering attending. When they walked into the chapel, someone was randomly playing *Let it Be* on the organ. Immediately, Luisa's mother said, "It's a sign" that her son should attend that college – which he did.

Years later as an adult, Luisa too started observing signs that had meaning and provided her with guidance. Throughout the process of recording her personal symbols in over 50 journals, Luisa has made sense of their meaning and has utilized them to help her take big steps in her life. She now wants to not only share her true stories with you, but also provide practical tips on how to spot your personal symbols and then use them to empower, inspire, and give you guidance on your journey.

Printed in the USA
CPSIA information can be obtained
at www.ICGtesting.com
LVHW071247190923
758537LV00006B/1170

9 781088 217894